PRAYERS
OF
HONORING

Written by Pixie Lighthorse

Lighthorse Publishing, 2016
Redmond, OR

I

© 2016 Pixie Lighthorse
All rights reserved.
Made in USA

Second Edition

Library of Congress Control Number: 2015944665

ISBN: 978-0-692-67536-6

Cover design: Morgan Wade
Layout: Twozdai Hulse

Lighthorse Publishing
SouLodge Ranch, LLC
Redmond, OR 97756
www.pixielighthorse.com

For Miles, Ivy and Sky, who
keep me on my knees in gratitude.

CONTENTS

FOREWORD

At a very young age, I became aware of my aloneness against the expansiveness of the sky. Grown now, this feeling persists, and yet I am not lonely. Contextualized by the vastness of the universe, and now the addition of my adult responsibilities, the largeness of life can sometimes swallow me whole. I can still feel small among the big, but I've learned to ask the Infinite for guidance.

Not long ago I asked for a teacher. I didn't want a guru, nor did I want my overwhelm to be exploited by another. I wanted direction without agenda. I wanted wisdom without losing the ownership I had of myself. I wanted my direction to come from the natural world and from my intuitive connection with it. I wanted assurance in my mind of what I already knew in my heart.

My own prayer led me to this book of prayers. In it, I found what I was seeking and more. I found inspiration, a guide, and a way of connecting with Spirit. I found a dependable reminder of my own relevance that didn't diminish the greatness of life's mystery for me. I found a teacher, and I found my own humble, human connection to the great web of life. My heart and soul have embraced this book like an old friend.

Because it is an answer to my asking, *Prayers of Honoring* reminds me of the fertile, listening nature of the universe. With its non-dogmatic voice, it beckons me. It reminds me of a time when "human being" meant inhabiting a natural and spiritual world that was as alive as a person's own body and greater than a person's own identity. It reminds me of a time of deep connection, when the natural forces of the world merged into everything and everyone, and people felt attuned to their sense of place and time. It reminds me to appreciate life's naturalness. It reminds me to reawaken that lost magic and to recreate that time here and now.

Prayers of Honoring is a more complete rendition of my heart's song to Spirit. Though we didn't make the prayers in each other's voices, somehow Pixie's prayers are mine and mine are hers. It turns out that all hearts seek a similar kind of embrace.

These are timeless and universal prayers. Since having the privilege of sharing them with my students and experiencing their responses, I see how they speak to others as they speak to me. Each prayer awakens and gives voice to the inner wisdom that is universally known.

Her book is an appeal to the spirit that exists deep within the heart of all beings. The magic in these prayers is a reminder of our need to call upon nature and Spirit for help. *Prayers of Honoring* can help us connect with what we are already part of. It can help us know the wild, the whispers, and the magic of life.

May we all thrive as keepers of the sacred prayers held here.

Annie Adamson
Founder of Yoga Union
Portland, Oregon

INTRODUCTION

Prayers of Honoring was written in the spirit of communion—of sharing from the heart with others during vital times.

In Western culture, we keep too many things to ourselves. Prayer, among other things, has become a private practice for those of us who don't congregate for spiritual purposes. Our language for connection to something greater than ourselves has become abbreviated to basic iterations and generalized affirmations. Perhaps this is so that no one will be offended by our approach, or so that our spiritual personalities—who we are when we talk to and reach for the Divine—can remain under a cloak of mystery and intrigue. Maybe it has something to do with our collective intolerance for vulnerability.

We speak of being "solitary practitioners," which to excess can be another way to justify isolation during times that cry out for community. This response comes from fear. In fact, the majority of people I have encountered in my circles express a deep and constant yearning for belonging and acceptance, which can only be enjoyed when we take the risk to be seen by others like us.

As an educator of creative, environmental, energetic, and spiritual possibilities, I think that our general practice of tolerance can be defined efficiently as our willingness to agree to disagree. Dig a little deeper and we find another definition of tolerance as simply putting up with something. Acceptance proves more worthwhile when we can welcome the full spectrum of languages and expressions that seek to connect us and others to the magnificent qualities of this mysterious existence on Earth and beyond. When we're open to receive the heart's intelligence, we offer acceptance to ourselves and others, shifting our patterns of isolation and loneliness. The challenge is to share ourselves, our words, our expressions, our art, without fearing we are doing it wrong. Connecting in spiritual community only requires that we bring the original essence of who we are to the conversation and welcome others in the same way. When we're willing to speak our hearts out loud, they can be heard.

Prayer is still very much a sullied concept. To some ears, the word results in triggersome personal, cultural, or collective memories. The sour taste of yesterday's experiences of over-organized religions, forced practice, penance, rigid disciplines bearing harsh consequences, heavy-handed authorities on the laws of God—all leave little room for welcoming prayer back into the heart, home, and psyche. It is my hope that we can overcome our prayer trauma and begin to speak the words of spirit from our hearts out loud again.

My inspiration for *Prayers of Honoring* is simply the awe of Great Mystery and the interconnectedness of every living thing. It must also be said that the book would not exist if not for my community of sisters, who asked for more each time I shared a prayer. Those who mother the world with their gifts of healing nurture provide needed sanctuary for others finding their sacred voices. I will be forever in awe of the power of those who gather to share their hearts with acceptance, vulnerability, and non-judgment of others.

Each day at work, I encounter nurturing mothers honoring their intuition rather than following socially prescribed, inappropriate, or outdated methods of parenting. I encounter women recognizing their deeply feminine natures, acknowledging the Earth as mirror for their immense beauty and creativity. I get to work with parents envisioning a safer, more honest world—who respect the divine nature of children and also accommodate our human mistakes and flaws, which are often our best teachers. I get to work with partners seeking new ways of communication that are truly fair and equitable. I hold circles of women befriending their shadows and learning to be still in their years-long healing process. I'm blessed to drum, sing, and pray with children who see the unseen and have their wisdom heard and understood. I work with men willing to stand up to the old regime of the patriarchy and courageously rebuild a culture around holistic values, integrity, love of the Earth, and generosity of spirit.

I wrote the prayers to honor the things that are easy to celebrate, and also those things that require more practice. It was written as a reminder of the critical importance of honoring, which is to show high respect. It's my thought that respect and reverence are missing from Western culture. To cultivate these things through the rhythm of prayer is to demonstrate devotion to the unfathomable energies that suspend us between the divine energies of Earth and Sky every day and night.

Each time my beloveds and I pray together, our hearts open a little wider. I get to know them in a new way, and what's stirring inside of us becomes known to one another. In the process of connecting to the Divine within and without, we get real with ourselves. It's in this peaceful practice that we come clean and say what we really mean. It's my belief that creating our own family and community practice of prayerfulness brings us closer to one another as we travel forth.

For my family, prayer is healing medicine. It can be made, offered, sent, embodied, and lived.

I hope that you enjoy this collection and find it inspiring for your own practice. Open it when you desire to connect to the Source of Life, which holds you, and allows you to float weightlessly without burden for a little while.

In reverence,
Pixie Lighthorse

HOW TO USE THIS BOOK

This book has many creative applications, and you will find your very own way with it. It is now in service to you as a tool for connection and to help your voice along where it may need a little support. It has a way of shapeshifting and changing when you're not looking. Prayers that didn't grab your attention the first read-through might strike a chord at unsuspecting times. You might wonder how you missed that one the first time.

Prayers of Honoring has traveled around the globe and fallen into the hands of many courageous and outspoken individuals and leaders. It's been assimilated into yoga teacher training curriculums and healing circles, read at workshops, demonstrations, and consciousness festivals.

This edition includes journal pages for you to write down your thoughts and prayers for yourself, your people, the coming generations, and the world. Use the blank pages to draw the images which are evoked by your thoughts and feelings. Allow this book to be a keeper of your sacred communion with the Source of All Life as You Understand It.

Another way to work with this book is to look through the table of contents and check in with what needs tending. What thoughts and sentiments are flowing through you? What is seeking expression and connection?

The twenty-eight prayers have been organized according to the seasons and the Four Directions. Each coordinates with an element and associated properties. You may find it inspiring to move through the prayers as one would the calendar year, noting what is present for you, especially during transitions.

Prayer is how we dialogue with a power greater than ourselves. Through the process of praying, we often discover what we are grateful for and what we would like support with. It is a gesture of opening the pathway for listening and channeling the next right action.

The process of connecting and communicating with what is moving inside of you, and through the cosmos, will strengthen your intuition; and that is a good compass to follow.

EAST

Season: *Spring*

Element: *Air*

Properties: *mind, new beginnings, birth, adventure, vulnerability, risk, sunrise, ignition, potential, visions, dreams, seed-planting, exploration of spirit, daydreaming, wandering*

Honoring Origin

It is a blessing to be alive today given the long journey through humankind's primitive beginnings to the present. It is a miracle that we are here. Help us to remember the value of our presence at this moment in time.

Rewind the lost tapes of our cellular memories to connect to our humble beginnings with awe. Lead us back to the time when we operated with our senses. Help us find our way without gadgetry and excess noise. We are grateful to hear. Sharpen our skills so that we may hear with our eyes and see with our ears. Help us with our night vision—for moving through darkness with courage. Spread our toes fully open to receive the energy of Earth through our soles.

Teach us to honor how the Moon illuminates the path of the night creatures and the ancient Questers, the Fire-Makers, the Seekers, the Seers-of-Stars, and the Record-Keepers. Help us feel the warm history of our ancestors, allowing it to inform us about our ways today. Put us on a good path.

Teach us how to walk in strength and beauty again.

Allow us to love the darkness—to wrap it around our shoulders, hunker down at the fire with it, and honor the wisdom that comes from time spent in the dark. Give us a cauldron to stir and the years and patience to wait for good brew. Help us trust that it'll all make sense in the end.

Help us surrender and feel everything, especially when we have nothing to comfort us and take the edge off. Teach us to understand that it is not beyond, but within our human chaos that calm directives are located. Remind us that enlightenment is sometimes come by clumsily, or revealed through a dusty dragging by the hair! Help us craft our own tools, which will illuminate where we've been so that we comprehend our personal evolution.

Help us value the muck we have had to crawl through to stand on our own two feet.

Allow us to celebrate where we're going, without forgetting where we came from. Shine your loving light on the rivers that carried us in—our family lines and the threads that connect us to our primitive beginnings.

Help us to awaken from the long slumber and bind ourselves to the magic of transformative evolution in a loyal union with you, embodying the fever of progress with clear intention.

Honoring Vision

We're here in gratitude for the blessing of life. We give thanks for the gift of sight, in all its forms. We know what to do; we just need a little reminding now and again. Standing in the East, we greet the new day—the promise of a great adventure. Find us on the precipice of fresh awareness.

Teach us to begin by caring deeply and to let that caring stretch out over the horizon on Eagle's wings. Show us how to take that step over the edge into the unknown: to remember that risk brings learning, even through our mistakes.

Steep us in the waters of trust, so that our toes will not be afraid to touch the mysterious future. Remind us that we are responsible for what comes next—that the past is a good educator, but not always a reliable compass.

Help us prioritize our health, the health of others, and the Mama planet. Help us organize and assemble, and share our ideas with one another. Help us to find ways to clear the obstacles that congest the pathways you're trying to reach us through.

Show us how to apply our caring nature to the world, so that it's a better place for people—a place where we love to live. Help us do our part to create that world. Here and now, help us envision it, without idealism and pretense.

Give us the strength and tenacity to endure, to show up at the town hall meetings, to do the inner housekeeping that allows us to make a difference for someone struggling the way we once did. Let us move into the next phase with confidence.

Ground us. Lift us up. Ready us for what's to come by putting our feet on the good path.

Help us to see with long vision before we set out, to remember the great, great-grandchildren who are coming, to keep their air and water clean: to spare them our shadows by doing our healing work now and walking our good walk.

Honoring New Life

Thank you for the abundant life force that pulses within us and enthusiastically welcomes the springtimes we are waking up to. It's a blessing to feel the warmth of the Sun on our heads and the moist soil of Mother beneath our boots.

Thank you for spotted fawns, for thorny asparagus, for peonies, for the promising snow melt, for cherry blossoms and new hashmarks on our growth charts. Thank you for fresh buds and green sprigs, for early birdsong and chittering squirrels. Thank you for renewing our souls with hope as the season turns over.

Let us think of every project as precious seeds. Guide our hands to plant with love, to water the rows with diligence and to treasure the sowing process as much as the impending harvest. May we plant with conscious intention. When we have a Very Good Idea, help our minds align with our hearts to know if it is the one to set in the soil. Let love drive the plow.

Help us see each other as your unique creatures, each of us with special gifts designed to honor life. Remind us to acknowledge and celebrate our innate talents—to find creative ways to celebrate the gifts you've given us in this lifetime. Show us new ways to express ourselves with more truth and clarity.

Find us lying on your breast, Mama, under the blue Sky Nation, sprouting with each raindrop, breathing what the plants breathe, seeing what the birds see, feeling what the rabbits feel, sensing what the snake sense Teach us to care for and preserve your invaluable resources so that the snakes, birds, rabbits, deer, and plants can continue to thrive, as well as the children.

Instill in us the belief that we can create a world we can be proud of, and leave the Earth more beautiful in the process. Work in our hearts so that we are open to sharing our harvest when it comes. Make good scouts of us, so that we can follow a path of bliss and leave no trace.

Honoring Lightness of Being

Thank you for this beautiful day of potential weightlessness and magnificent connection. We're blessed to have the opportunity to travel light: to be relieved of our burdens with the help of Divine hands to rest in.

Show us the sacred in everything. Help us to recognize it in the simple things. Direct us on how to let the old fall away: the old ideas, the outdated patterns, the heavy resistances, the obsolete models. Allow our stripped-down, winterized minds and bodies to feel the sensation of new buds, new life, solar energy. Impregnate us with the electricity of your Sun, the shock of your lightning, and the promise of your rich Earth. Help us contain the pollen-like reserves that lead to bursting into full bloom.

Hold our little hands when we're uncertain and don't wish to let go of what has become so comfortable, but can be so heavy. Bathe us in deep trust of your infinite Mystery. Baptize us in the waters of One Love. Remind us that we are mirrors reflecting each other like wild prisms, refracting one another's lights. Remind us that what we share comes beaming back at us. Let us be your Rainbow Makers.

Adorn us with our microflight superhero capes, our robin's egg blue caps of intuition, our soft-walking-on-the-earth shoes. Expand our capacities for kindness, for love, for compassion, for receiving, and for letting you in through every pore to mingle with our beautiful, fumbling humanity and give birth to our divine wisdom—your gift to us. Let us unwrap ourselves in the season of new beginnings with ease.

When boulders appear on the path, help us roll them away to greet the illumination at the end of the tunnel. Untether our recurring accumulations of stones from our backs, and let us become accustomed to traveling light, like Butterfly.

Honoring the Elements

We are so profoundly grateful for our full-spectrum lives today: for the restoration of life that happens when we travel our circular, spiral paths.

Thank you for instilling in us the call to adventure, and for the lure to presence the Light like fancy-winged moths to flames. Thank you for each tiny grain of sand, each crystalline star, each prismatic tear, each mountain we've climbed, each ounce of primordial muck we've had to crawl through to get to this place.

Bless this day in which we breathe deeply of your sacred air, dance around your sacred fire, cleanse in your sacred waters, and rest peacefully on your sacred Earth. Remind us, when we call in your help, to be very specific—that the powers are listening, and that every fulfilled request results in an impactful ripple. Help us to think ahead before we put into words what we think we need.

May we know the whole truth about ourselves and believe that this knowing, followed by our efforts today, will unfold seasonally, with patience and grace. Teach us to honor the alchemy of the elements and the natural cycles.

Show us how to stand strong and face the world together. Remind us of all of the help available to us: found in the vast sky, the tall flames, the infinite sea, and the deep soil. Help us walk your transformative wheel of life over and again with joy for the experience of practice. Remind us that we are not alone by revealing to us our holy compass and by directing its holy needle.

Allow us to be courageous when walking in our glorious labyrinths; as we come to understand your visionary nature, your fiery nature, your fluid nature, and your grounded nature; as we attempt to follow your lead through our darkness.

Honoring the Spark

Thank you for this beautiful day of creative fire. We're so grateful to be alive and seeking wellness together. Light in us a great flame of understanding.

Amplify your radiance throughout our energy centers when we hesitate and doubt. Let us be lanterns for your cause.

We see your beauty, Sweet Spirits, reflected back at us in the tiny new flowerheads and shimmering puddles. We recognize new life everywhere, and in it our own capacity to blossom and radiate life energy, too. We feel the warmth of your subtle sunshine and can be confident that we warm the hearts of others when we shine our lights, acting as the generative and magnificent instruments we were designed to be.

We know that creativity is the way. We hear your call to make beauty in the world and leave a trail of rainbows in our wake. Help us to face our challenges head on with innovation; help us save this beautiful Earth Mother and ourselves by our wits, by our willing hands and hearts. Help us to value that we are living organisms here who can give back as much as we take.

Remind us of what ignites us, what inspires us to mimic your minute-to-minute acts of Creation. Give to us everything we need to believe in miracles and magic, and the patience to wait for them to unfold in front of our apprehensive eyes. Show us how to stay lit as we come out from our dark caverns of fear. Release our trepidations and put your creative power to work in us. Move our hands across the paper, our brushes across the canvas, our bows across the strings.

Infuse our weary hearts with the faith we need to carry forward—not like soldiers warrioring tirelessly for the cause, but like lightbeams who have already reached their destination before our minds can even imagine it.

Honoring Germination

Thank you for this miraculous day of reckoning. Thank you for your unpredictable weather, which allows us to stay aware and awake, tuned in, turned up.

Bless the soil today for all of the little promises held safe in its loamy fecundity. Show us that we, too, are this procreant.

Bless the hillside fires that burn in holy honoring of the heat needed to hatch the seeds of the future.

Help us stay awake all night to tend the coals of possibility.

Help us to make out the dancers in the flames.

Show us how to move our bodies like fire.

Hold us high in our fertile possibility; strike the match that re-lights our sacred inner lamps, which grow dim during cold, bleak times. Free us from the paralysis resulting from circular arguments that play over and again in our minds. Remind us to get out of our heads and get outside, rain or shine! and shout our gratitudes for being alive under the first hot sunshine of the year.

Awaken in us a ferocity and fever for what we know we are passionate about, but haven't yet found a way to express. Balance us with gentleness so that we handle the fragile with care. Help us tone our discernment so that we know where to go when the road forks and our roots split in two. Help us to make repairs where needed, in the time required for wholeness.

Give us the visions and lead us to the people and the wise inner guides who will help us give birth to our best ideas. Prepare us with faith for our pregnant days to come. Let us know that we can do this! Reinforce us for the coming season of planting and later, the harvest. Remind us to think about what we want to reap, so we can sow right.

Humble us with your divine magic, which allows all things to grow.

TURNING TO THE EAST
FOR SUPPORT

A new beginning is on the horizon. Step out with trust, and greet your blank canvas.

New beginnings are honored when we celebrate the beauty of what is about to be, but is yet unknown. Energy gathers, and warmth spreads under your feet, readying the trail ahead. What aspects of your original essence can help you understand your purpose? What fuel do you need for the journey?

Imagine yourself empty of all previous experiences, and connect with your higher mind rather than fear, which has the power to stop you before you begin. What innate characteristics are you being called upon to develop or strengthen? What preparations are needed? What first steps can you take to get started?

Take an inventory of your situation. Look around at what you see. If you could pack only a small suitcase for your journey, what would you want to be sure to carry with you? What kind of support from companions do you require to stretch yourself beyond your perceived limits? What permissions do you need to give yourself?

Our connections to those who came before us can be powerful motivators. Even if you did not admire them in life, what qualities stand out that could be of help to you now? If the ancestors could re-name you based on your highest potential and essential purpose, what would they call you?

Create an intention to honor your spirit's purpose. What wants to be born? What have you intuitively always wanted to do, say, or make? What long-reaching effect would the birth of such a thing have on humankind?

Anxiety is now a part of our daily language to describe our fears of the future. What frightens you about what might happen if you take a risk? How will you feel if you remain safe in your comfort zone? When did your fear develop, and how have you successfully overcome it in the past to get where you are now?

Trust is essential before setting out on any new adventure or task. What is your relationship to trust and faith? How were you cultured to trust? What

helps you to cultivate an attitude of trust today?

SOUTH

Season: *Summer*

Element: *Fire*

Properties: *body, movement, manifesting, taking action, activity, creating, gathering, assembling, building, expediting, tending, celebrating, a sense of being on fire*

Honoring Purpose

Thank you for the blessing of breath, of hydration, of animation. What a joy it is to be alive and living with intention.

Direct us to our solemn devotion; help us to be receptive when you call. Awaken us to that which is greater than the daily lives we're carrying on with right now. Create in us a chain reaction of events that find us centered in the current, headed for our destiny, and able to read the roadsigns. Teach us that each of us is full of beautiful gifts to be shared and how to be open to receive. Remind us with great frequency that what we enjoy most can be aligned with what you have in mind for us, if you can help us with our listening.

Show us that what we're called to do is not only possible, but that it is our duty to honor our sacred work in the world. Point us to the resource that will support our efforts.

Help us to know that we can do it.

Walk us back to our wildness, where we can become clear, in our feral states, about what we need to do and how we need to be. Split us open at the beauty-point, where our abilities meet the energy of our hearts. Crack through us with your lightning bolts, and allow us to channel your divine electricity into all that we do.

Help us to be conductors.

Purify us with your rain, and awaken us with your thunder. Rock us to peace after we've thrashed against the trust that we are safe, sheltered, seen, heard and held, and then put us back on path. When we are prompted to leap, hold the net for us. We'll need it.

Help us to dive off the precipice, knowing that you will be there to guide our next right step.

Hang us gracefully upside down to gain perspective, so that we may know ourselves, our work and you, from every angle, with the love only you, the Divine, can inspire.

Help us to take a chance on ourselves.

Honoring Freedom

Thank you for this beautiful day of growth, of separation and individuation. Thank you for showing us how to love and to also be free.

Thank you for the water, the grass, the simple things we need to live and tend to take for granted. Thank you for wide, open-range thinking and for the ability to create our own realities with your help. Thank you for the courage to step off the well-traveled thoroughfare to seek our own fortunes of the spirit.

Bless our paths as we leave a season of our lives behind and declare new footsteps, once again, as you have blessed us so many times before now. Bless the Wheel that keeps us turning and learning. Guide us to autonomy as we learn to make spirit-stuff our first priority and the closest matter to our hearts. Let us allow this in others, honoring their way—knowing that we each have our own sweet language with you.

Guide us to true freedom by showing us our part in everything—everything beautiful and of creation, as well as that which is unseemly and destructive. Both are of you. Allow us to sit on the edge of the cliff for as long as we need to before we can move forward. Keep us from hurrying the process, knowing that it is in our readiness to leap that we gain our sovereignty. Remind us that it is ownership of the role we've played that will release us and forgiveness of ourselves that sets us free.

Humble us by removing our disclaimers, our qualifiers, and our blame of others for putting us in this place. Find us sitting on the mountain waiting for the visions to come from you, disrobed of our arrogance, stripped of our expectations, devoid of impatience. Surround us with your magical animals, vegetables, and minerals, which support our earth-walk toward full flexibility. Show us that it isn't others who hold us back, only ourselves and our very good reasons. Show us another way.

Hold us tenderly when we suffer, and amplify our radiance when we shine. Heal us with right medicine, which opens us all the way up, in full support of our sensitive natures.

Teach us to nurture ourselves deeply and leave tracks for others on path to find us and their freedom, too.

Honoring Resources

Thank you for this holy day of plenitude. Thank you for every crust of bread and every loving nod.

Help us in every way to give back more than we take.

Thank you for lizards, like tiny dinosaurs, who catch flies on the kitchen floor and show us that we can abandon and regenerate our tails when in real danger. Thank you for the teachings of the ancient dragonflies: proof that fairy realms do exist. Thank you for the elders who have not a minute of life-energy left for superiority or ego and who lead with grace and humility. Keep putting them on our paths. Keep our mouths more closed than open and our eyes steadily connected when they speak. It will be our turn to speak soon, and let us be wise, too.

Lead us to water, and allow us to drink deeply. Cause us to remember the waters from which we came and how precious the water is today: once a free and clean necessity, now peddled in plastic bottles for several dollars each. Teach us how to protect her flow. From that, we can learn to respect the flow of our own feelings, which have become stagnant from dishonoring and depression. Help us step into her current and navigate her precious highway.

Do not tolerate us when we hop from consciousness to unconsciousness. Wink at us in your magical way to call us back. The sunflower, which blooms just once, spreads a mass of seeds and contains the intelligence to keep the life cycle going with full presence and no regrets. Help us to nourish as many with our goodness. Refresh our memories of the importance of continuing to evolve, and not attempting to prolong the inevitable. Let our wisdom flow forward to quench us later in life. Show us, by all means necessary, that there is no going back to sleep once we have been blessed with sacred awareness.

Show us the rain and the rainbows. Send forth charitable spirits to keep company with. Remind us every day that there is no such thing as 'our people' and 'not our people'. Everyone is our people, under one Sky, on the breast of one Mother. Teach us to honor the stones, plants, trees, and creatures as our kin, knowing that they wear such disguises so as not to frighten us with their power. Let us be open to their teachings. Employ us as their protectors, their voices, their stewards.

Help us, in every way, to give back more than we take.

Honoring Community

Thank you for the ones who find their way to our sides: our brothers, sisters, tribes, and clans. Thank you for the willingness to take care of one another and value our contributions as a whole. Help us to put the good of the whole before the good of the few.

We need your support, as we take the next steps, to expand. Ease our fears, and teach us to gather in a circle of equals. Remind us that a circle has no beginning and no end, and that nature contains innumerable examples of the beauty of co-leading and the sacred geometry of many parts working as one.

Manage our defenses; diffuse our bombs; humble us so that we can tune into your Divine frequency again and hear each others joys and cries. Impart to us immense tolerance for the eccentricities in one another, knowing that we have them, too. Strengthen our connections, and bring us together like family.

Remove our irrational fears of moving along the road together, and allow us to look at all options for teaming up. Inspire in us the creativity required to dream outside of our insular boxes and single-family homes, and instead meet up at the fireside to break some bread together and spread our beautiful ideas out on the table like a feast. Lean us into one another's shoulders when we need a little care.

Fill us with unassailable HOPE that our collaborations will yield great harvests.

Humble our pace with patience for each other. Slow our progress when we need to take a break to truly appreciate it and understand the consequences. Clear our injuries so we can hear just what's being presented today.

Teach us to barter and trade for what we need. Show us new ways conducting of community and commerce that benefit our higher purposes and our fellowship. Remind us that not so long ago, our currency was simply trading our best work for someone else's to meet our needs.

Burn up our excess ego, and inspire our communications with thunderous compassion. Provide us with the strength of character needed to be good to each other.

Let us default to great love in times of doubting ourselves and one another as we work together toward solutions.

Honoring Right Medicine

Thank you for this resplendent day, bursting with healing possibilities.

Let us get drunk just on your love today. Set our anxieties free on the knowing breezes of your Mystery. Share your sweet language with us so that we can speak softly to ourselves in our healing processes.

Be a reminder to us, above and below us, to hold sorrow and grief in one hand and great wisdom and joy in the other. Teach us how to make room for both in our hearts, knowing that we cannot deny either of them. Bring our hands to our hearts in honoring of the way we've matured in acceptance of this truth.

Guide our sweet hands to flush our false medications and step toward the real medicine—the triple crown of divinity, humanity, and the pure energy that electrifies and animates everything. Whisper to us the truth of what is real, what to tend, what to feed, and what to pay attention to. Sometimes we forget.

Align us with your sunrays, your big waves, your cumulonimbus clouds. Put us in the direct line of action. Give us the awareness to know that our way has been prepared for us. Give us the courage to face it. We are open to receive from you, and even before we feel fully steadied we will begin giving back in gratitude and service. This we promise.

Remind us that many medicines that are right for others may not be right for us. Help us to discern what heals us, which words work for us, what levels of closeness are healthy, and that right medicine is the kind that helps us to make commitments that serve us, as well as the purpose much greater than ourselves. Helps us to set healthy boundaries and also invite our vulnerability into our intimate unions. Remind us that our own tears grant access into our hearts. Let us have at least a few who get to see us soft.

Bless all of the mothers and the fathers who brought us here. Bless their shortcomings and oversights, and help us to forgive. Show us that our hurts were inflicted by those who were hurt, and guide us to heal so that we can stop those legacies from passing on again. Show us that what hurts deeply today is most often what hurt tremendously long ago. Give us the skill and the hope to make a new way for ourselves.

Instill in us the divine gift of care, that we may extend our compassion to all who live.

Honoring Ebb and Flow

We honor our lives today by wading knee deep in the Light of your reflection. We are grateful for the uneven tides, which keep us on our tiptoes in the constantly moving sand.

Inspire peace in us, and help us cultivate trust that all is as it should be, as it was meant to be, even when we're treading water. Teach us to float effortlessly when the waves threaten to take us out one last time for good. Help us learn that it is surrender held in tandem with our best effort that puts us on the right path.

Help us, Wise Ones, to understand our true needs, so that we can reciprocate the generosity and abundance you give so freely. Teach us to see, to read the tracks, to follow the markings that lead us to the healing places. Remind us that loss is just as powerful a teacher as gain. We know that we can learn to love both. Hold us in our suffering when we don't understand.

Help us to claim our grief and show others that we can make room for theirs, too. Remind us that there is no such thing as personal pain: that we all experience suffering, and that it is meant to be shared.

Allow the forces of nature and Spirit to guide us to what we want, and help us learn the acceptance to receive exactly what we need. Pull us in and push us out; agitate us gently to keep our cells turning over and the knowledge fresh. Brush off our accumulations and attachments at just the right time—when something unknown is coming in.

Show us how to walk in a meander, or in a straight line, or even backward: whichever serves our highest potential. Even a freefall can be medicinal at the right time.

Find us tabling our resentment when it's time to step back and observe, assess, and replenish our reserves. Find us in a flow of love even when we are silent or holding ourselves at a safe distance.

Help us feel our way through this day, giving and receiving love from you and those who surround us in a beautiful ellipse of reciprocity. Show us how to balance the doing season with rest, and grant us permission to plug into the Great Source for much-needed rechargings.

Let us give thanks and get our knees dirty making offerings for grace.

Honoring Surrender

Thank you for this reflective and contemplative day. Thank you for contrast, so that we can be clear of where we are, Great Ones.

Help us to surrender.

Send the flood of salty tears when it is time to acknowledge and release. Let the rivers flow from us, creating movement and health in our watery bodies. Conspire to also deliver friends, visions, dreams, music, and healing food.

Help us to surrender.

Show us how to give in and not give up. Remind us that there is a time to make decisions and there is very much a time to sit with strong feelings and patiently await the decision making time. Witness us leaning our swords and spears in the corner to rest a while.

Teach us to cleanse out old ideas, old expectations, old patterns, old triggers, and old bad habits, which harm us and linger in our bodies with symptoms indicating spiritual illness. Guide us to heal utilizing the old ways, which do work and have been forgotten. Send us the spirits of our grandmothers and grandfathers with wisdom from the Other Side of the Mountain. Help us welcome them and all of the Helper Spirits into our sacred spaces.

Help us to surrender.

Let the waves overtake us and spit us out on the open sea, so that we may know both the depths of our own Mystery, and how the Mother holds and nurtures us, even when it feels like we are drowning.

Be a reminder to us that the skin we shed today will feed the soil, and that the shell that protects us can crack and crumble into useful organic material—an offering to the Earth for her willingness to do our composting.

Help us to surrender.

Empty us out, and fill us back up with what has always been ours and decidedly of you.

Allow us to revel in the beauty and nakedness that surrender brings.

TURNING TO THE SOUTH
FOR SUPPORT

A fire is burning inside of you. Acknowledge your momentum, and let one right action prompt the next.

Once you recognize that your journey is underway, it is important to see where support is needed and ask for help. Which resources haven't you considered yet that might be vital to your success?

Our lifetimes are aflame with skills, magic, and medicine. What are your strengths, and where do you think you fall short for this undertaking? What tools have you forgotten you have access to? How resourceful do you see yourself? What have people historically counted on you for?

In a state of expediting, it is easy to push beyond one's capacity. What will help you achieve balance in your body and prevent a state of overdoing? How can you activate and support your body's optimal function at this time?

The body and all of its valuable parts help us to bring a vision into reality. What story is your body telling you that desires attention? What stresses can be eliminated to create a favorable environment for growth?

Where we put our energy determines the outcome of our journeys. What activities and thoughts support your creative processes? Can you tap into where your energy is most abundant and utilize it as fuel? Follow the threads that point to fulfillment, and determine which aspects you require council around.

What we put into our minds and bodies has the potential to sustain our higher levels of doing and making. What medicine energizes and nourishes you? Are there any habits that might need to change or shift?

Collaborating with others can yield fruitful inspirations for your process, whether moving from one job or home to the next, creating a body of artwork or music, or moving through the stages of grief or divorce. Who would you love to join forces with? Who might you benefit from sitting at the feet of? Is there a dream mentor or guide you have been wanting to work with?

It is easy to get caught up in expediting and forget to celebrate and honor the little successes. What are you building? Does it honor who you are and your intentions? How can you take some time to pause and celebrate that you are

living true to your purpose?

WEST

Season: *Autumn*

Element: *Water*

Properties: *emotions, feelings, releasing, surrender, grief, harvest, ancestors, maturity, voice, healing, tears, flow, cleansing, clearing, engaging the spirits, overcoming obstacles, forgiveness*

Honoring Descent

Thank you for this stunning day of opportunity to stand at the well. Staring down into the hollow tunnel, let us feel our fear about what awaits. Let us lean over the edge, knowing that you hold the golden rope, and then let us fall...

Today we walk in the darkness. Magnify your shine up above, as we lower ourselves down. Fine-tune our night vision so we can sense each possibility that comes before us, each path a milky way in our periphery. Teach us, through the process of descent, how to be initiated into the clan of Having-Been-There.

Open our floodgates, with the knowledge that our tears will cleanse the toxic build-up of unexpressed feelings. Help us to acknowledge the pain of generations behind us, and our power to heal it when we agree to take the journey down. Remind us that our tears and perspiration are our natural cleaners. Help us honor the tools we were born with to express our sorrow and transmute that which is held inside of us too tightly.

Allow us the grace to choose our words with care, to pick our battles down there wisely, and to harvest our own medicine from the depths. Allow us the opportunity to come up for deep breaths in between our descents into the Underworld for reflection. Hold our hearts while we do the work in pitch-blackness, on the hooks, undergoing the little deaths we know are necessary for rebirth.

When it is time to return, call us back. Extend your hands to us, and touch our hearts, so that we will rise and step forward more awake than before. Infuse us with life energy, which spills over in abundance to our sisters and brothers who are in need of a power boost. Remind us of how much to keep for ourselves so we can stay in flow and continue in our work as generators.

We ask all of these things with respect and admiration for the universal and omnipresent awesomeness of You and the darkness that cannot be avoided. Keep us safe when we must go there.

Honoring Grief

Thank you for this blessed day: this blessing of life on us, heavy with awareness of what has been surrendered.

Inspire us to grieve enough. Remind us not to strive for completing the process for the sake of being done. Help us with our tendency to avoid. Establish in us a belief that we get to wear the face of our pain, not a brave mask that puts others at ease. Help us to speak and honor our pain, understanding that we do not suffer our losses alone. Ease our minds when those who cannot relate to our suffering don't know what to say or do for us. Hold our rage and abandonment while we come to discover what is at the bottom of our deep sorrow. Emphasize to us that someone, somewhere understands, despite our contrary thoughts.

It is a comfort for our hearts to be able to access the spirit of what is no longer. Unlock the passageways so that we may commune with those we remember. Allow the souls who have been reclaimed to visit in our dreams and visions. Help us to preserve the love we came to count on. Teach us to honor our relatives who have taken on another form with purpose and reverence. Instruct us in the art of divine communication.

Remind us that everything that dies will be reborn in some way, even if we do not possess the words to describe this process. Help us trust in your Mystery while we feel our feelings. Groom us to take the long road if we need to.

Help us know that our tears are cleansing and our grief sacred—that we can take all of the time we need to release and cleanse our wound of loss. Point it out, each time we forget that we are equipped with the perfect tools for this process. Give us the energy and strength to weep.

We're grateful for the visceral experience of flow when your healing rains wash over us, allowing our emotional bodies to be washed in your waters. Carry our honest pain downstream to join the infinite tributaries of sorrow and mourning in the salty womb of the Ocean. Let us mingle our tears with others in a gesture of sharing. Show us how to honor our collective human experience.

Remind us that we do not have to fill the empty places with anything at all at this time.

Guide us gently through the anxiety of vacancy where love once held us.

Honoring Release

We're so grateful for this deeply precious life. Looking around, we see your love in all things. Allow us to feel more blessed than baffled, more clear than confused, and to let go of the ropes we've bound so tightly around our own fighting arms.

Help us shed our armor and release the sticky mortar that binds us to our broken thinking. Melt our pitiful pasts away and off of us so that we are solid in the present and bright for the future. We're ready to allow your radiance to rub off on us.

Hold us tenderly when fear arises in us: when the voices that plague us take over. Let us look at our lineage and our unwanted patterns, and cut the cords. Give us the courage to stand up for ourselves. Help us face off with that which still hurts—with a power that only you can provide and that no human reasoning can eliminate long-term.

Encourage us to allow our mistakes, and help us to find relief from our humanity in your divinity and our connection to you. Remind us of the strength and beauty of each delicate fir needle, each sharp-pointed cactus spine, each sting of the scorpion's tail, each disappearing snowflake—that we may understand and appreciate our need to protect and preserve. Allow us to rebirth in sacred silence, shedding that protection and inviting growth through vulnerability.

Help us to build the fires of purification up on the hillsides. Help us stand the sticks up tall and straight. Throw our excess into the mighty flames, and take our prayers for a new way up to the heavens. Let us remember that when we give our excess to you, it is transformed into new life.

Help us to remember that we contain the tenacity to overcome, as modeled so beautifully by the Earth and her obvious evolutionary and cyclical processes. Teach us to love the life-death-life cycle and to know that what harms us will fade into the ashes, if we can bring ourselves to let go.

Honoring Forgiveness

We are blessed to be alive today, standing in our full beauty and height.

Thank you for the signs, the bleach-white bones, the love notes filled with sentimental hints that life is short. Thank you for holding us during the string of attacks, some of which relentlessly throw us up on the rocks and pull us back out to sea. We're grateful for the calm moments and for the Sun, for the washes of the light of understanding, which come unexpectedly and straight from you, often at unremarkable times.

Teach us how to forgive and leave the past in right time. Help us savor the present and release the need to know how it'll all turn out. Hone our trust, our trust, our trust, that difficulty today will become ease tomorrow. Find us leaning into you, knowing that our judgments and grudges are contaminating our precious blood and life-force, and that only by releasing them will we find peace. Let us give our grievances to you.

Remind us of what really matters at the end of a day; give us rest in the knowledge that it will all work out. Let us consider ourselves Beloved and walk in the direction that leads to respect for ourselves and for your presence in our lives. Let that respect inform our choices about how to handle ourselves when we're in conflict with others. Allow us to locate the Divine in ourselves, so that we may know that we are of you and able to channel your grace on demand, through our diligent learning and devotion to the goodness that lives inside of us.

Remind us frequently to own our part in a matter, to become humble in your presence, and to hold ourselves to a higher level of accountability. Move our hands to build the altars and create the ceremonies that call in the spirits for assistance. Remind us of the importance of thanking them for their divine services.

Show us that we can believe in your magic and your perfect timing. Help us acknowledge it all and to cut strings when needed.

Honoring Rites of Passage

We are spilling over with gratitude today for divine support and presence in our lives. We need your energy to move through our transitions. We need creativity and motivation to find the healers who can help us honor ourselves when we change.

Help us to cherish the inevitable changes we face. Guide us in ceremony and celebration when our time comes. Teach us to honor the young ones when their bodies and minds shift and mature. Show us how to midwife the elders and the sick across the bridge and into the next dimension.

Hold us close to you when we must leave old ways behind to embrace what is next for us. Remind us that change is not to be feared, but cradled in recognition.

Channel our new energies into the causes that serve the highest purpose for all. Teach us how to understand that we are all the same in the way that we continue to develop, up and away, like magical beanstalks. Help us to transmute what falls away from our strong stems, in order to mulch and protect what is trying to grow from our roots up into us.

Break down the dams of resistance, which obstruct the steady current between our minds and our spirits and You. Help us to surrender to wonder during our transformations.

Help us clear the way for beauty, in all its forms, to stream through us. Root us firmly in the soul-soil as our branches reach high for home in the Star Nation. Lay us down on the Great Mother, under your sparkling blankets and the comfort of the moon, to receive your transmissions.

Surround us in your warmth and light, and usher us into our new stages as precious children of the Earth, who never stop growing, and do so because you inspire us to rise.

Honoring Wisdom

We're so grateful for our precious lives, mysterious forces of enlightenment.

Your sage direction is channeling clearly. We are listening. Open us even more. Bow us down to the bewildering magic of All That Is. We are hungry to rise above fear and feel the gifts of our suffering with wide-open hearts. We are ready to sharpen and soften, all at once. We are ready to be like the Old Ones from the dreams we are trying to recall.

Please help us to hold ourselves in high integrity, so that we can shed all that keeps us from experiencing intimacy with you and with our loved ones. We know that it is through deep compassion, respect, and love that we become wise. We understand that it is love, not knowledge, which begets intelligence. Help us to grasp that we must do this for ourselves before we can truly love others and the world.

Guide us to hear with the echolocation of Bat, to comprehend the resonant truth, leaving no room for doubt about the next right task. Increase our abilities to perceive authentically. Let us do this during dark times—the wintertimes of our lives.

Grow us, and evolve us, like the ancient creatures who have come from Mother Ocean's saltwater wombs. Put us back in touch with our sweat and our tears and the embryonic waters of life. Receive our weepings as an offering to you.

Show us how to use what we've got to get to where we're going. Remind us that it's all within us, right now. Help us pull through the eye of the impossible needle and be victorious in our flexibility. Humble us now more than ever.

Lead us toward our deepest healing and elevated understanding, so we can climb the mountain of our highest potential.

Allow us to be bold in our expression of love for you and for one another, taking away all hesitancy and resistance, in order to become who we've always been.

Honoring the Perfection of the Universe

We have so many names we call you and ways in which we contact you. Thank you for answering to them all, though you are truly unfathomable and nameless.

Your infinity is beauty uncontained: the most precious kind. Teach us how to release our desire to know everything about everything. Take away our desire to perfect others or change them. Instill in us the wisdom to accept what is good enough on any given day.

Let us hear your voice in no language we can really comprehend. Let us grow comfortable with your ambiguity. Remind us that you are always in perfect order, even though we cannot perceive it.

Your Sun is a mirror for the Light that lives within each of us. Show us how to channel that energy through us and keep our hearts warm for lovers, for children, and for strangers, too. Let us have no need to know why, just to know that love is light.

Remind us how to walk as a blessing between the heavens and the landscape, always ready to jump into the wind, with wildish roots under our bottoms, as the feathery flowerheads of the dandelion do: not asking questions about their destiny, but simply admiring their lightness and willingness to sail through the skies.

Inspire us with your exquisite impeccability, because it allows us to forgive one mistake after another in ourselves and others, forever. Show us your spiral, never-ending brilliance, like tiny treasures we can hold in our hands, to grasp you for only a passing moment. Hold us as tiny treasures in your magnificent hands.

Remind us—with the stars found inside every apple, with every nut housed inside of its protective shell, with every perfect purple plum—that nature, all around us, shows us the divine.

Tickle us awake from our ignorant slumber by helping us remember the sweet soul song you taught us before we were born: the one the stars are singing for us right now.

TURNING TO THE WEST
FOR SUPPORT

In the dark and watery depths, you can gain understanding of that which must be healed and released. Dive down and honor your qualities of fluidity.

At some point on our paths, we come face-to-face with our obstacles and are called inward to investigate. Are there ancestral or recurring pains that show up as obstacles on your path? What persistent griefs appear and reappear for you?

The inner, emotional life is an integral part of what determines our happiness with the entirety of the life we are living and creating. Which emotions rise up for acknowledgment and get inadvertently pushed back down by the part of you that doesn't have the time, energy, or resources to deal with them? What flood gates will open if you give voice to what still hurts? What adversity do you have around showing emotions? Have you been cultured to believe that crying is a negative response to pain and suffering? What seems impossible to change?

Throughout life we have learned to love and appreciate some things about ourselves while others we wish would go away. What we dislike has a way of showing itself, and the more we try to shove it down, the more it fights to be heard and understood for what it really is. These "shadows" can be acknowledged at a deeper level as developing in childhood for our survival. What of the shadow-self would like to be healed?

Often what trips us up is an unconscious unwillingness to look at what we don't like about ourselves or our lives. Regrets and shames haunt our dreams and prevent them from being realized. What can you forgive yourself for? Have you made amends to those you have hurt? Have you asked others for forgiveness? Have you grieved your heartaches enough?

At this stage in our adventures, it is common to feel utterly alone, and even to push loved ones and life away in order to affirm this thought. Can you call upon your ancestors for strength during difficult times? Can you be willing to release what has become toxic within you? Imagine that they have hired you to do the job of cleaning house for your lineage. What support do you need to clean, clear, and cleanse your precious system and your family line of limiting beliefs?

NORTH

Season: *Winter*

Element: *Earth*

Properties: *spirit, honoring elders, rest, observation, stillness, dormancy, preservation, wisdom, gratitude, clarity, death & rebirth, inventory, responsibility, celebration, oneness, completion*

Honoring Divine Presence in All Things

Thank you for this bright day. Thank you for putting out the call to come home to you.

Help us sing your songs of love and devotion to our understanding of you loud and clear. Help us write those that live inside of us, remaining unspoken and unsung. Remind us that they are there because you are there.

Let these illuminated occurrences, these brief seeings and believings, be a map to our self-Knowledge and self-Trust, as well as reflective of our faith in your magic. Show us everything that is beautiful, and also help us to appreciate that which is furthest from beautiful for the lessons that accompany it. Let nothing be lost on us. Make us your sensitive trackers, seeking truth and finding it tucked away in the unexpected.

Let us channel your pure energy so that we can feel you in everything. Show us how to bring it in as often as possible, providing us with reserves for staying fueled for human tasks. Remind us that time spent with you is what recharges us best.

Draw sacred hearts on our souls, leaving us with no question about our lovability and value. Show us that you are here in every lily, lake, and lover.

Help us recognize your unconditional love—we promise to let it ripple out far beyond us once we connect with it.

Lead us into a practice of valuing our serenity above all else, so that we may learn the true meaning of conserving what is precious. Help us to agree on what that is. Teach us how to walk through the world consuming less and caring more about the spirit that lives in everything.

Show us how to be generative and not deplete ourselves, nor others' energies.

Honoring Lineage

Thank you to the Ancestors for bringing us through your sacred line. Thank you for lifting us up above our family's suffering by helping from the Other Side. We feel your presence all around us.

Send in the birdsong to lift us to our higher frequency, so that their lively, cheerful trills and tweets stir us awake from our slumbers and put us in direct contact with you. Let us feel your good vibrations spreading through us like a herd of wild horses.

Let us carry forth a good legacy to mother the children, honor the elderly, and celebrate the lives of those who are leaving this dimension bound for the next adventure. Help us not to fear the death of ourselves and loved ones. Be our insurance. Keep in touch.

Come to us in dreams, and empower who we are, how we walk, what we speak, and what we do with your spirited knowingness from the Other Side of the Mountain. Teach us all of the ways to connect with you, helping our arms reach back for you for reassurance.

Walk with us toward joy, because we need you when we struggle. Help us in all the ways you couldn't when you were here. Help us to lay down our burdens, and to trust that we don't have to fight so hard anymore, because of the battles you fought for us long ago. Help us make sense of the stories—plentiful and sometimes tragic. Show us how to connect the dots.

Be the rocks we can climb up for a better view and crawl into for shelter. Show us the right medicine for our families and exactly how to administer it. Give us more reasons to grow our faith, because we humans are very forgetful creatures. You remember what it was like.

Help us tune into your station and we'll blast it.

Honoring Divine Stillness

Thank you for every beautiful day of the week and the hellish days, too. Thank you for chaos, so that we may know disorganization as a friend and motivator, and find peace there. Thank you for urging us to create time for sitting in it.

Lead us to the trailhead to take the quest: to find the Holy in the Mother, the burning bush, the light at the end of the tunnel, the golden fleece, the dragon guarding the treasure, the pirate's booty, the White Stag, the reason Why.

Help us take the journey and sit down for many rests along the way.

Help us to get quiet, so we can feel our soul-salt coming to the surface to be known. Send in Fox, so we can follow in her noiseless footprints to the place in the forest where the din of civilization has died all the way down. Help us remember the way to walk efficiently and stealthily until it is time to rest.

Find us sitting at the base of the inexhaustible life-tree, which whispers so softly that we must learn a whole new way of listening in order to hear its messages clearly. Flash us your lightning to keep us awake and lucid, because it is difficult not to fall asleep when we are learning to still the active mind.

Help us to breathe in the unknown and breathe out peace with what will come.

Condition us in the ways of placidity. Float us on the lake when there's no breeze, so that we may come to center-pointedness. Plant us in the desert sand like a flag of completion, just for a little while: until the guardians of the East call us forth into action again. Let us always remember how to come back to this place.

Teach us that after we've walked without sound for many miles and sat listening for many more... then it will be time to share the story.

Help us find access to your pure calm inside of us. We will know it when we feel it, like a loving hand over our hearts.

Honoring Leadership

Thank you for this holy day that is rising. We are nervous, but we can step up. We have reservations, but we have your support. Sponsor our causes when we find a good way.

For the sake of our precious, short lives, make leaders of us—because, after all, we are here. We are all ears. Guide us to study the chemistry lesson for living from our hearts and allowing the ripple to flow out and into our communities. Teach us right messages. Give us the foresight to understand the consequences of our works and actions.

Help us with our confidence.

Drench us in your abundant fragrances, and drape us in ferns and forest mosses so that we may know the pleasure and joy of setting verdant examples. Muddy our shoes, so that those in our footsteps leave behind perfection in favor of adventure and the exploration of new ways. Let us show up not as stoic, humorless presences to those learning and watching, but allow them to see us in our humble states and able to turn difficult situations around on a dime when that's what's called for. Help us do the best we can and make the best of challenging situations.

Help us put our hearts on the line.

Hold our hands as we unfurl our teacher's wings. Unleash the songs in our hearts, and carry our melodies over the mountaintops and through the snaking rivers, cleansing and opening those who hear them. We know that open hearts are what heal the world, so let us open, open, open.

Reveal our souls to us so that we may know ourselves and understand what is needed.

Put us in front of those who want to listen. Work with our tongues and our paralyzed voices to clear the way, so we can say what needs to be said.

Honoring Oneness

Thank you for another beautiful day on Earth. Today we are the same, every one of us.

Thank you for the opportunity to make our Earth a better place to live and be and for the children to inherit. Please show us how to slow the damage we do to you, Mother. Work your magic in the hearts of those who are working hard to reduce consumption, pollution, contamination, overuse, and violation of your precious resources. Work even bigger magic on those who don't see the effects of the human lifestyle on this planet. Work deeper still to unite us in these causes.

Allow us to be as One—one civilization suspended between you, to erase the lines that limit us to our country, our ethnicity, our continents, our towns, our histories. We are all citizens of the world and can improve the way we move around on you when we can utilize your love story, Grandparents of Creation, as inspiration for living. Help us to live into that.

In our self-reflections, make your presence known. Show us that you are here with us. Let us see the soul in all things and honor ourselves. Let us see each other as you see us. Let us make our human mistakes and learn divine self-correction on our road, leaving the conquering and divisiveness behind.

We call upon you to help us lighten our loads so we can fuss and fret less over things that don't really matter—to lighten our hearts so that we can let more love in and out. We ask you to brighten our awareness with your divinity so that we can see where we can grow beyond our limitations. Some of us see you in different ways, so make sure you appeal to our senses and awaken as many of us to your love as possible. All of us. One human being at a time. Show us how to inspire each others' awakenings and support one another under not-so-ideal circumstances.

Protect the little ones from harm. Lead us to new ways of guiding them that transcend the painful ways, the neglectful ways, the manipulative ways. Show us how to guide them with nurture and compassion.

Help us see the beauty in all living things and lessons and make the world a better place by doing so. Help us be the beauty you intend us to be for all.

Honoring Equality

Thank you for this exquisite day of promise and equilibrium. Thank you for the opportunity to tilt the scales with the wisdom of our experience.

Find us honoring the men, boys, fathers, brothers, and sons who surround us. Let us lift them high up to the Sun in respect and love so that they may find their way in a world that is trying so hard to come into balance with the Divine Feminine. Let them know that we support them, accept them, and love them deeply. Inspire in them a willingness to work together with each other and with women.

Find us honoring the women, girls, mothers, sisters, and daughters in our lives. Let us ground them on the Earth and in their beautiful flesh, in all shapes and forms. Help them to honor the Divine Masculine within them, so that they can protect themselves in real danger and expedite the jobs. Assemble circles of women so that they may gather and make the good medicine. Align them with men in one beautiful purpose.

Mother Earth, find the people laying on your surface for comfort, climbing your trees for the gift of overview, and calling your nurturing energy up through the soles of their feet, in a gesture of accepting your deep core medicine, too, alongside the masculine energy of the Sun.

Show us the animals, plants, and stones that are medicinal for our earthwalks. Allow us the strength and courage to lay down our bones, and those of our loved ones, when it is time to return spirit matter to the Sky Nation and earth matter to you.

Hold our hands as we take this journey together. Show us ourselves in the mirror of one another, and allow us to own what it is in others that we, too, contain.

Bestow upon us compassion, tolerance, the knowledge that there are many, many ways to bring you into our hearts and heal what is broken and what still hurts.

Curl us up in the season we reside in now, so that we may know and feel your warm and omnipresent love.

Honoring Completion

Thank you for this bright day of transformation and of finishing what we started. We're proud of what we've created and lift it up to you in honoring.

Give us today the ability to leave the shells of ourselves behind. Impart in us a strength for the unknowns to come, so that we are fortified for the next leg of our journey. Show us our inventories with clarity, so that we can move forward clean and clear. Allow us our satisfaction with all that we were able to do and crystalline awareness of the legacies we are leaving in our wakes.

Support what is delicate in us—our tender and holy geometry, which is still sensitive to everything in the environment, even after such miraculous, evolutionary adaptations. Sharpen our perceptions, and heighten our readiness for what's to come. Remove our fears, which keeps us one-dimensional and our souls frozen in time. Witness our rites of passage. Let us revel in what we have made with you in our hearts.

We call upon you as humble humans wanting a safer home here on Earth while we're here—a place where the creatures' numbers are in balance, your air is nourishing, and your waters cleansing. Show us how to create this for ourselves and those who follow our generations. Inspire our smaller footprints, so that when we are complete and death is at hand, we are ready to move into the next dimension with peace in our hearts.

Witness our unfinished works, our half-written poems, our stalled letters, our crumbled relationships, our abandoned canvases, and let us meet them near the finish line. Put the brush back in our hands, place our minds back at the negotiation table, help us hold the frightening pen, so that we can know the joy of seeing our creations through.

TURNING TO THE NORTH
FOR SUPPORT

High on a mountain-top, you can reflect quietly on what has become complete. Wear your decorations of actualization proudly.

Honoring a cycle begins with becoming still, resting in the memory of experience, and accepting what has taken place. Each detail is meaningful, even if simply to be given a nod and released. How do you want to know others? How would you like to be known?

Building community and relationships connects us to our warm and transformational natures among others. What did you give? Who did you give to? What responsibility did you fulfill?

Wisdom emerges when we engage our ego-strength, meaning that we are willing and able to hear feedback and manage our emotional triggers with awareness. In what environment do you feel most grounded? How have you been successful at getting your message across fairly and clearly?

Your gift of observation means that you can see many possibilities within a situation. How can you implement a slow and steady process of finding guidance? Where can you sit in stillness while you wait for wisdom to come to you?

Much of our cultural standard lacks in rites of passage. Transitions are moved through thanklessly and unrecognized. What has not been honored of you and your life? What ritual or celebration can you create to raise the level of appreciation for all that you have been and done? Who would you want to be there? What would you like to be remembered for, and how?

Accountability to future generations is part of our work. Going forward, how can you utilize your gift of conscious oversight, compassion, and empathy to ensure that your choices have a responsible impact? How can you honor the medicine of the grandmothers and grandfathers to bring about a promising future for the young ones? What needs to shift, and what part do you play?

Let's be sure to take the time to honor ourselves and the people in our lives on occasions other than births, marriages, retirements, and deaths. In what ways do you like to honor others? How have you celebrated the good work of others and their lives? Who do you know who would benefit from being lifted up and acknowledged?

GRATITUDES & ACKNOWLEDGMENTS

This sweet offering would not have been possible without the expert teamwork of Twozdai Hulse, Morgan Wade, and Stefanie Renee Lindeen, to whom I owe a deep gratitude for helping me grow up with my work, and for believing in me and always being right there with great ideas and creative problem solving.

Many gratitudes to Annie Adamson (Yoga Union Portland) for putting this book to work in her teacher training program and for honoring me with the new foreword in the third edition.

For carrying me through the toughest year of my life: I am deeply grateful for the holy trinity of Jen Gray, Kolleen Harrison, and Melody Ross.

For being voices in my head at all the right times: I am ever-grateful to Christine Mason Miller, Stephanie Ladd, Maya Pagán, Maya Stein, Tingle, Jennette Nielsen, Sunjay Owen, Diane Marshall, and Irene Skau.

I owe the greatest debt to my parents, Nan and Donnie Carr, for their faith and unwavering generosity, for helping me to do my very best in all things. Thank you for teaching me how to take care of myself and my babes, and for always being willing to roll up your sleeves and get your hands dirty for family.

I owe the sweetest kindness to Sky Sharp for praying together with me, reminding me of the power of connecting aloud and taking a chance on love, in spite of his cowboyish, maverick, lone-wolf ways and despite my gun-shyness. Thank you for absconding with a dark gypsy, as your lineage seems to be famous for.

Thank you most of all to the spirit of Great Mystery and to my Ancestors, who came colliding full-force into me in a nearly-unbearable and shocking white light during one of the most painful blindsides of my life. Thank you for refusing to leave. Thank you for filling my heart with forgiveness and tolerance, and for continuing to lift me up when I was getting so good at falling down. Thank you for making communion with you easy. Thank you for making yourself visible to me.

Made in the USA
Lexington, KY
25 October 2017